Oven Mitts
to die for

Oven Mitts to die for

AND HOW TO MAKE THEM

by

Diane Wallis

The Watermark Press

ACKNOWLEDGEMENT

The 'Mind Games' mitt on pp. 36–9 is reproduced
courtesy of Annette Wallis, who was responsible for
its concept, design and pattern.

First published in 1998 by
The Watermark Press
PO Box 63 Balmain NSW 2041
Sydney Australia

Project Editor: Diane Wallis
Consultant Editor: Annette Wallis
Photography: Simon Blackall
Design: Sheringbone
Pattern diagrams: Diane Wallis

National Library of Australia
Cataloguing-in-Publication data

Wallis, Diane.
    Oven mitts to die for : and how to make them.

    ISBN 0 949284 34 3.

    1. Needlework. 2. Handicraft. 3. Footwear. I. Title.

746.4042

Produced by The Watermark Press, Sydney
Typeset in 12/16 pt Perpetua
Printed in Australia

Our Menagerie of Mitts

INTRODUCTION

Oven mitts, pot holders — whatever your preferred expression, these humble kitchen articles of cloth, usually padded, protect the hands when removing hot utensils and containers from the stove top or oven.

The history of oven mitts is hardly rich or detailed. To date, I have found no reference to these items in any tombs of the Egyptian pharoahs or seen any examples of Roman mitts perfectly preserved after the eruption of Vesuvius at Pompeii in AD 79. The busy-fingered, all-male knitters of the Middle Ages, famous for the stockings (hose) they made for lords and soldiers, seem to have overlooked oven mitts altogether.

Mostly practical and plain, oven mitts have had an occasional brush with embellishment in the past. Some vintage knitting and crochet patterns for fancy oven mitts are still in circulation. They were intended as gifts with a purpose for deserving mothers, aunts or grandmothers, or as stock for the handwork stalls at fund-raising fêtes.

Craft publications have always included a mitt or two for light relief from major needlework projects that require a lifetime of dedication. It is quite possible that craft editors' quests for arresting ideas for simple kitchen accessories have influenced the commercial production of oven mitts. Today, novelty mitts with three-dimensional waiters and bereted Frenchmen are mass produced and on sale at kitchen and homewares stores around the world. But who could be satisfied with the banality of mass production when the creative spirit beckons?

Oven mitts are fun to make because they are small and therefore quickly completed, and this book reveals that they are coming out of the closet in glamorous new guises. For what is an oven mitt but an empty canvas begging for a few strokes of brilliance. And here are seventeen, fresh from the oven of invention, employing a broad range of favourite handcraft techniques.

PRACTICALITIES

The most basic type of oven mitt is nothing more than a piece of fabric or towelling, ripped to a convenient size. The square model composed of two or three layers of stout fabric, with its edge neatly bound with bias binding and some sort of loop at one corner to hang it from, is the next step up the evolutionary ladder.

From here, we move to the more sophisticated double version of the aforementioned which is joined on two adjacent sides so the hand (which enters the mitt on its diagonal) is enclosed and better protected from heat.

A variation on the double version has a rectangular layer which is decorated; the hand is inserted in the centre of one side of the square and the hand spreads out from side to side instead of corner to corner. This version affords the oven mitt artist the chance to create within a landscape format.

The double-ended type is a popular style with the two hand pockets at either end of a padded and machine-quilted strip. With this design, it is important to make the padded strip long enough to reach comfortably around your largest oven dish or you will be engaged in a dangerous tug-of-war with yourself when safe conveyance from oven to bench is the aim.

Then there are the mitts proper. Those with the thumb extension on the underside are suited to the left or right hand. With the thumb to one side, if there is decoration on the back, the glove becomes suited to one hand only.

A frying pan in the oven is always a trap for the unwary; grab at the handle with a bare hand and you will reel back in pain. A well-padded handle holder that slips over the hot handle is one solution. Or you can even out the heat load by supporting the pan from beneath with one hand (protected by a mitt or cloth) and taking hold of the handle with the other equally well-protected hand.

In a commercial kitchen, hot utensils are quickly transferred from heat source to heatproof surface, in shielded hands. Woven cotton or towelling oven cloths used by food professionals often double as all-purpose wipe cloths. So they are always close at hand, they are 'worn', tucked into the long apron ties which encircle the cook's girth. When every second counts, there is no place for a 'right or 'wrong' side of a oven mitt, or any kind of decorative touch to cheer up the chef. These are luxuries only to enjoyed at home.

OVEN MITT MATERIALS

Fabrics and padding used in the construction should be washable. I used quilter's laine as the padding material because I had some in my sewing chest, but polyester wadding, cotton wadding, towelling or rags are equally suitable for oven mitts.

The thrifty housewife of yesteryear saved worn clothing and bedding (especially old blankets) and stitched them into oven mitts. Discarded clothing is still an excellent source of mitt material. I dipped into my rag bag and found fabric for several of the models featured in this book.

Pilled and worn-out machine-knitted woollens are also good for oven mitts because wool is a natural insulator. Either use the fabric for padding or as the external covering, but be aware that the hot wash in your washing machine may matt the wool.

Most of the materials in the oven mitt collection in the following pages came from the stack of fabrics and unfinished symphonies in my sewing chest and knitting hamper. It is a great relief to reduce the bulk a little and finally air some of the treasures that have been stored for years.

Although the giraffe print furnishing fabric is really far too precious for an oven mitt, it was great to find a use for this scrap left over from an upholstery project of the past.

My daughter's woven name tags, remnants of her school days, had been stored in a button tin for more than twenty years. Now at least some of them have been incorporated in a handle holder for her Le Creuset frying pan.

Hopefully, you will be inspired to look at what you have at hand and reassess the fabrics and wools in your own life, and view them as potential grist for your very own oven mitt mill.

CONSTRUCTION TIPS

When making oven mitts by sewing machine, be careful not to build up the layers to such an extent that the machine needle breaks with the effort of piercing the fabric. You can trim away the padding from the seam allowances prior to stitching so there is less to sew when binding edges with bias strips. When the oven mitt has a definite back-of-hand side (called the 'back' throughout the instructions), this does not have to be nearly as thick and heatproof as the front. Remember to build up the layers on the palm of the mitt where they are most needed.

A walking foot attachment on your sewing machine is a great help when sewing through many layers. It feeds the top and bottom layers into the path of the needle equally, so the top layer is not stretched out of alignment with the bottom.

Fusible web is one of the great inventions and greatly simplifies machine appliqué. It is fused to the underside of the appliqué pieces, and must therefore be cut as a mirror image (flopped or flipped) of the fabric piece. Because it is almost transparent, some people prefer to work from mirror-image patterns, tracing directly onto the paper side of the web. The web is then fused to the wrong side of the fabric and the fabric cut out around the edges of the paper.

Many of the patterns given here are also placement and embellishment guides, so mostly they are the right way. The crab is the exception because it is just one piece. With some projects, such as the coffee pot, I fuse uncut pieces of web to the backs of fabrics, trace and cut out the pattern piece and then place that on the right side of fabric and proceed with cutting out.

Baker's Delight

At a bakery open to the street, I saw a baker taking trays of hot bread out of the oven with both hands very effectively protected by the very simplest kind of oven cloth. Each was a piece of towelling, torn to slightly larger than hand size. A 'wristband' had been slashed close to the edge of one side, in the middle. The hand was threaded through this band at the top, over the back of the wrist so the palm of the hand was protected by the remaining towelling. The cloths dangled freely from his wrists when not in use, but could be quickly returned to the working position for the next 'hot' task.

The baker seemed quite attached to his towelling flaps, jiggling them playfully as he whistled and worked. Pavarotti hankies for the working man perhaps?

The version photographed is much more complex than this, but the materials have very humble origins. The towelling is the remains of an old, frayed bath mat and the white hand-print appliqués are from an old housework glove cut in half.

INSTRUCTIONS

Materials (for 2)

2 pieces of towelling, 23 cm x 50 cm (9 in x 20 in)
2 pieces of towelling for padding, 20 cm x 22 cm (8 in x 8½ in)
1 cotton housework glove
heat-fusible web
monofilament thread
white thread
blue knitting cotton
darning needle
60 cm (24 in) white cotton cord

■ Carefully cut seam from housework glove with small, sharp scissors to create two 'hands'. Press flat with a steam iron.

■ Place one of these hands, right side down, on photocopier. Cover with dark paper — a brown paper bag is ideal. Photocopy the hand.

■ Cut out the hand image. Flop it over, wrong side up, on the paper side of the heat-fusible web and secure with pins or adhesive tape. Draw around the hand with pencil and cut out around the line.

■ Lay fabric hand on the ironing board, wrong side up, and press fusible web to it, paper side up.

■ Peel paper from underside of hand and centre on a 23-cm (9-in) side, 2.5 cm (1 in) from the edge. Press to adhere.

■ Thread top of machine with monofilament thread (adjust top tension if necessary), adjust stitch to a narrow, short zigzag and stitch hand to towelling around its edge.

■ Fold towelling in half across its length and mark with pins; open out again. Centre a towelling padding piece on the inner face of the unappliquéd side. Pin in place, thread top of machine with white thread and secure padding with straight stitching around its edges and across both diagonals.

■ Refold assembly in half as before, with padding enclosed. Match raw edges and pin.

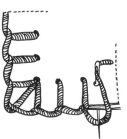

■ With darning needle and knitting cotton, stitch around edges and folded side with blanket stitch (see diagram).

■ Cut cotton cord in half, determine correct amount needed for 'handle' and trim to fit, allowing for a knot and 2.5 cm (1 in) unravelled tassel at both ends. Align knots with wrist of appliqué and hand stitch over the blanket stitched edge.

■ Make a second Baker's Delight.

Coffee Pot

Light plays on the faceted sides of Italian coffee pots in a most intriguing way. To capture the essence of the image and make this an easy project, I simplified it considerably. Starting with a snapshot I enlarged it on a scanner, printed it out, traced over the basic outlines and used this as the pattern.

The appliqué is done in six different fabrics with the purple also used on the business side of the mitt and the orange background fabric cut on the bias just for fun (see note). The appliqué pieces are fused in position and then secured with transparent thread and tiny zigzag so that the anchoring stitches are little more than a slightly textured, colourless line.

When assembling the mitt, the order of stacking all the pieces prior to sewing ensures that there are no raw edges on the wrong side.

INSTRUCTIONS

Materials

scraps of light grey, mid grey print, navy, dark navy, and black fabric

20 cm (¼ yd) of 90 cm (36 in) wide purple fabric

60 cm (⅔ yd) of 90 cm (36 in) wide orange fabric

20 cm (¼ yd) of 90 cm (36 in) lining fabric

fusible web; fusible wadding; wadding (batting)

monofilament thread

orange & light blue thread

wool and string for a knotted loop

CUTTING OUT THE MITT PIECES

■ Trace over or photocopy the three pattern pieces for the mitt on the following pages and cut them out. Note that the largest piece is called the Back because it covers the back of the hand, the piece with two curved sides is called the Palm/Thumb and the remaining piece with the curved top and straight bottom is called the Front.

■ From the purple fabric, cut one Palm/Thumb and one Front.

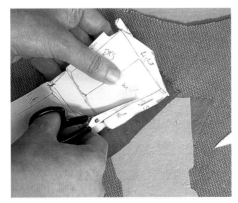

■ **1.** Cut out a full coffee pot shape in light grey and fuse to fabric as a guide. Then cut up the pattern, one appliqué piece at a time, place over appropriate paper-back fused fabric and cut out with small, sharp scissors. Fuse in place with steam iron.

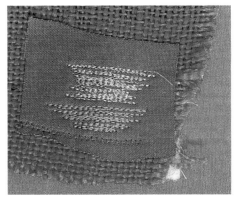

■ **2.** I was tempted to use silver thread on the purple band to suggest sheen on aluminium. On a test piece, I felt the light blue thread looked better.

From the orange fabric, cut one Back on the bias.

From lining fabric, cut one Palm/Thumb, one Front and one Back.

From the fusible wadding, cut one Back.

From the wadding, cut a double layer of Palm/Thumb and a single layer of Front.

PREPARING THE BACK FOR THE APPLIQUÉ

Place the orange fabric over the fusible wadding, fusible side up. Match raw edges and fuse by pressing with steam iron.

APPLIQUÉ

Press fusible web to the underside of the appliqué fabrics, first judging from the appliqué pattern approximately how much you will need. Be generous with the grey because the appliqué is built up from an all-over coffee pot shape in light grey.

Trace over or photocopy the coffee pot appliqué pattern and, using small, sharp scissors, cut out the coffee pot shape minus handle and knob. Pin this to the right side of the fused grey fabric and cut out accurately. Remove pins, peel away paper from underside and centre the shape on the orange fabric. Press with an iron to fuse.

3. Completed coffee pot appliqué with photocopied pattern and the original snapshot.

4. Stacking order before sewing the Palm/Thumb and Front.

■ From the coffee pot pattern, cut away the spout segment and pin and cut a spout from the mid grey print. Unpin, peel away paper from underside of fabric piece, position on appliqué base and steam press in place.

■ Continue in this way across the top of the pot from right to left. When the paper is peeled away from the beneath the fabric, the exposed surface is slightly tacky, which facilitates accurate positioning.

■ Cut and fuse light grey pieces over the light grey base for the lid and side segments. (I left the base showing beneath the centre band because it was getting too fiddly.)

■ Position and fuse the dark navy centre band before the purple centre band (which nearly obscures it), leaving only dark navy 'shadows' above and below it. Then cut out and fuse the black handle and knob.

■ Thread top of machine with monofilament thread (adjust top tension if necessary) and stitch around all the segments with tiny zigzag.

■ Change thread in top of machine to light blue (adjust top tension if necessary). On the purple centre band, between the mid grey printed segments, straight stitch backwards and forwards laterally to imitate the sheen on aluminium.

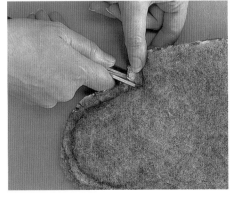

■ **5.** After sewing seam around the thumb and side extensions, clip corners, clip curves and trim seams.

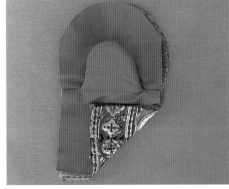

■ **6.** Turn through to right side to make the Palm/Thumb/Front assembly.

ASSEMBLING THE OVEN MITT

■ Stack in this order (from the bottom up) with thumb at top and raw edges of thumb and side extensions matching: 1. Wrist front, right side up; 2. Palm, wrong side up; 3. Palm padding; 4. Palm lining, right side up; 5. Wrist front lining, wrong side up; 6. Wrist front padding

■ Pin around the thumb and side extension seam, baste if desired and remove pins; stitch on machine with 10 mm (⅜ in) seam. Clip into corners, clip curves, trim seam, turn through to right side to make wrist front/thumb/palm assembly.

■ Stack in this order: 1. Back, right side up; 2. the previous front/thumb/palm assembly, lining side up; 3. Lining for back, wrong side up.

■ Pin, baste if desired and remove pins; stitch on machine with 10 mm (⅜ in) seam. Clip curves, trim seam, turn through to right side to make oven mitt assembly.

FINISHING THE LOWER EDGE

■ Cut 5 cm (2 in) wide strip of lining fabric long enough to fit around the base of the oven mitt, adding seam allowances to both ends.

■ Fold lining strip in half with wrong sides together and seam short ends together to form a loop. Press seam open.

■ **7.** Stack in this order before sewing.

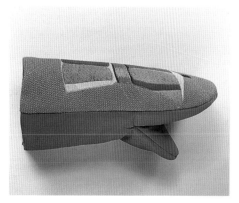

■ **8.** Side view of the completed unit.

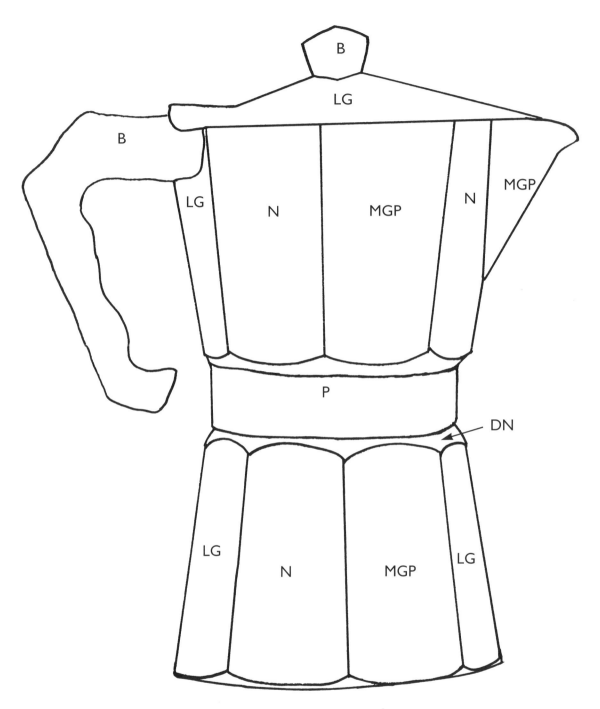

KEY FOR COFFEE POT APPLIQUÉ DIAGRAM

B = black
LG = light grey
N = navy
DN = dark navy
MGP = mid grey print

▨ Fit loop over base of oven mitt, right sides together, seam in centre of oven mitt front and raw edges matching. Join with a 10 mm (⅜ in) straight stitch seam.

▨ Press under a 10 mm (⅜ in) hem on raw edge of lining strip. Press lining strip inside the oven mitt and secure with hand or machine stitching.

▨ Make a knotted loop over a circle of firm string (see diagram on page 103) and hand stitch it to the side seam of base for hanging.

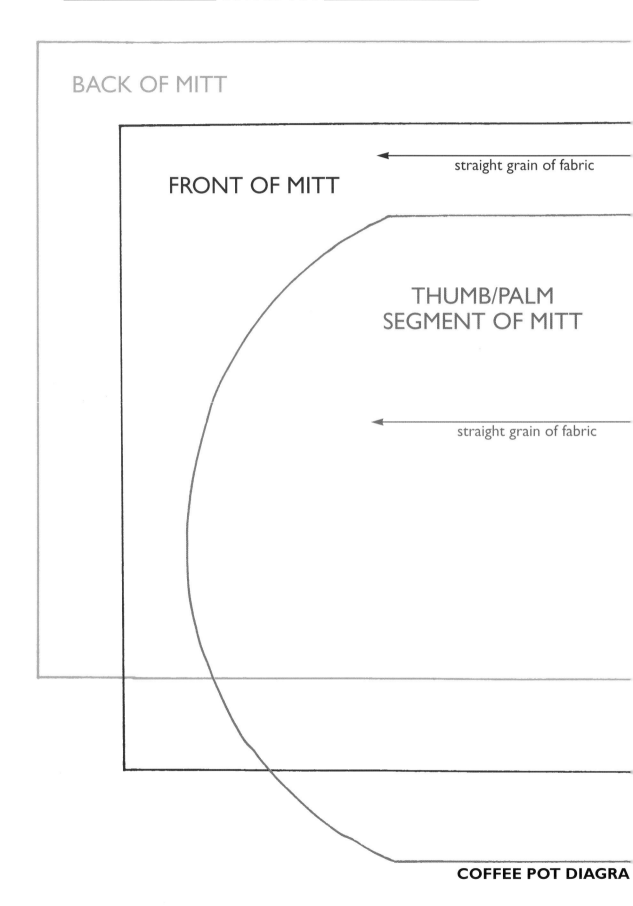

BACK OF MITT

FRONT OF MITT

straight grain of fabric

THUMB/PALM
SEGMENT OF MITT

straight grain of fabric

COFFEE POT DIAGRA

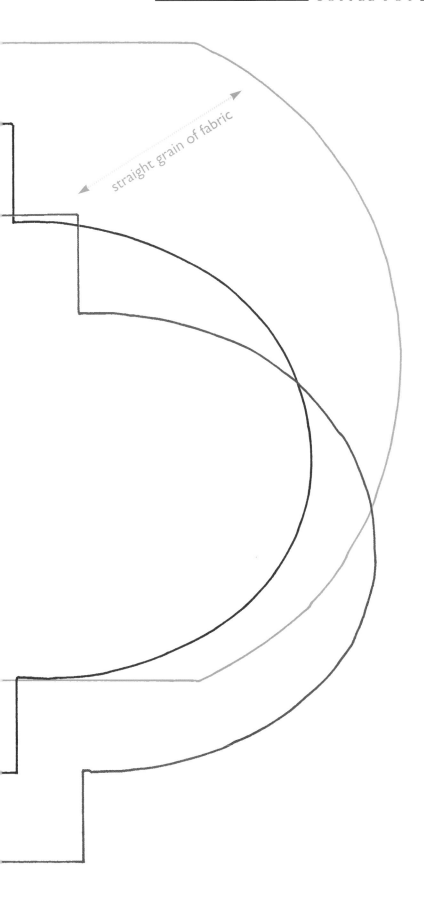

straight grain of fabric

Crab Claws

This crab appliqué came from an abandoned unfinished wallhanging of an underwater scene once intended for a child's room, so the creature was already fused onto its brown background. I particularly liked the way the orange velvet of the crab's carapace had buckled when it was fused to the background. As I stitched it down, to my delight, it buckled further. A real mud crab has these same undulations on its shell.

The image was a little small for the oven mitt, so I added a fringed fabric 'napkin' (which was extracted from a book of fabric samples) in the loop corner.

Back (with appliqué and called back because it encloses the back of the hand) and front (plain and padded) are made separately, then joined with binding.

INSTRUCTIONS

Materials

18 cm (7 in) square of orange velvet for crab

30 cm (12 in) square of brown fabric for background

28 cm (11 in) x 12 cm (4½ in) piece of checked cotton for fringed napkin

1 m (1 yd) green cotton poplin for lining, back and binding

fusible web; 23 cm (9 in) of 4 mm (⅛ in) thick fusible wadding

wadding (batting); monofilament thread

green thread; brown thread

embroidery hoop (inner hoop bound with tape to prevent fabric from slipping)

dressmaker's pencil; 2 small black beads for eyes

CRAB APPLIQUÉ

▩ Trace over crab diagram onto the paper side of the fusible web. (The crab image has been flopped in the diagram to give the correct orientation on the finished appliqué.)

▩ With steam iron, press fusible web to wrong side of velvet. With small, sharp scissors, carefully cut out velvet crab. Peel paper from back of crab and steam press velvet crab on right side of brown fabric using photograph as a guide and noting that finished mitt is around 23 cm (9 in) square.

▩ Place brown fabric, face down, on ironing board. Centre fusible wadding over it (fusible side down) and fuse with steam iron and pressing cloth.

▩ With top of machine threaded with monofilament thread (adjust top tension if necessary) and using a tiny zigzag stitch, sew around edge.

▩ Change thread to brown (adjust top tension if necessary). Place brown fabric in embroidery hoop with crab centred and with right side of fabric over outer ring, then press inner ring into outer ring and adjust screw.

Change to embroidery/darning foot, lower feed dogs, set needle to straight stitch. 'Thread paint' with free motion machine embroidery outer edges of crab, leg segments and blanket stitch effect around front and sides of shell. The hoop, guided by your hands, determines stitch length, direction and density. Keep the revs up on the machine and move the hoop slowly. You develop a rhythm after a while; it's a bit like drawing with a fine pen.

■ Cut, pin and machine stitch green lining to the appliquéd Back around edge.

■ Fringe one long and two short sides of the checked fabric. Pin it around what will be the loop corner, making random pleats along its unfringed side and machine stitch in place.

PADDED FRONT

■ Cut two 23-cm (9-in) squares of green lining fabric and two squares of wadding.

■ Sandwich the wadding between lining, match raw edges, and pin.

■ Machine stitch through the assembly from side to side in any desired pattern of repeated lines to quilt.

■ Stack and pin Back and Front together, matching raw edges. With scissors, trim corners to make them round, unpin.

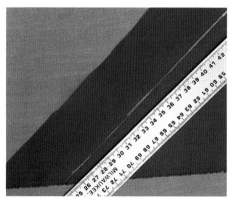

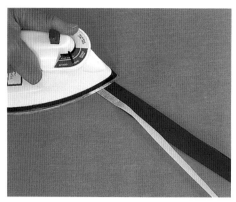

■ **1.** On the bias, rule and cut 5-cm (2-in) wide strips of fabric.

■ **2.** Press bias strip in half and press 10-mm ($^3/_8$-in) strip of fusible web to its fold side — wrong side of binding.

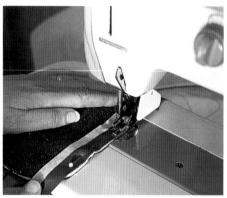

■ **3.** Stitch binding to right side of work, right sides together and raw edges matching. A walking foot prevents the layers from slipping out of alignment.

■ **4.** Binding has been stitched around a corner.

■ **5.** Fold binding over to the underside and press in place with a steam iron. Do straight sides first and ease corners with fingers before finally pressing.

■ **6.** With monofilament thread in the top of the machine, stitch in the crevasse when the binding and brown fabric meet. This is an invisible line of stitching which firmly anchors the binding on the underside.

BINDING THE EDGES

■ To find the true bias of a length of fabric, take one corner of the cut edge to the selvedge on the other side, keeping the other corner constant and using the fabric's width as the radius. The fold is now at a 45° angle to the selvedge and the fold is on the true bias. Iron the fold flat and use this as a guideline from which to cut bias binding. Rule lines using a steel rule and a dressmaker's pencil.

■ Cut bias strips 5 cm (2 in) wide. If necessary, join them along the straight grain of the fabric.

■ Fold bias strip in half along its length, and press fold with a steam iron.

■ Cut a strip of fusible web 10 mm (⅜ in) wide the length of the bias strip. Fuse it with a steam iron to the fabric along the fold line. Leave the paper in place. The side of the bias with the fusible web is the wrong side.

■ On the Back with the appliquéd side up, pin bias binding strip around the two adjacent sides of the loop corner, raw edges matching and right sides together.

■ On a 10 cm (4 in) piece of unfused bias strip, fold under long sides so they meet in the middle, press and fold again (in half, lengthwise). Stitch close to the side folds to secure. Overlap ends to make a loop and pin to the underside of back, raw edges matching.

■ Stitch 6 mm (¼ in) from the edge, easing around the corner and catching in the loop on the underside.

■ Peel paper from the fusible web. Fold binding over to the underside so that the folded edge of binding with its strip of sticky web just covers the stitching just completed. Press in place with a steam iron; do straight sides first and then ease in the corner with your fingers before pressing.

■ Thread top of machine with monofilament thread and have thread to match the lining in the bobbin. On the right side, stitch in the crevasse

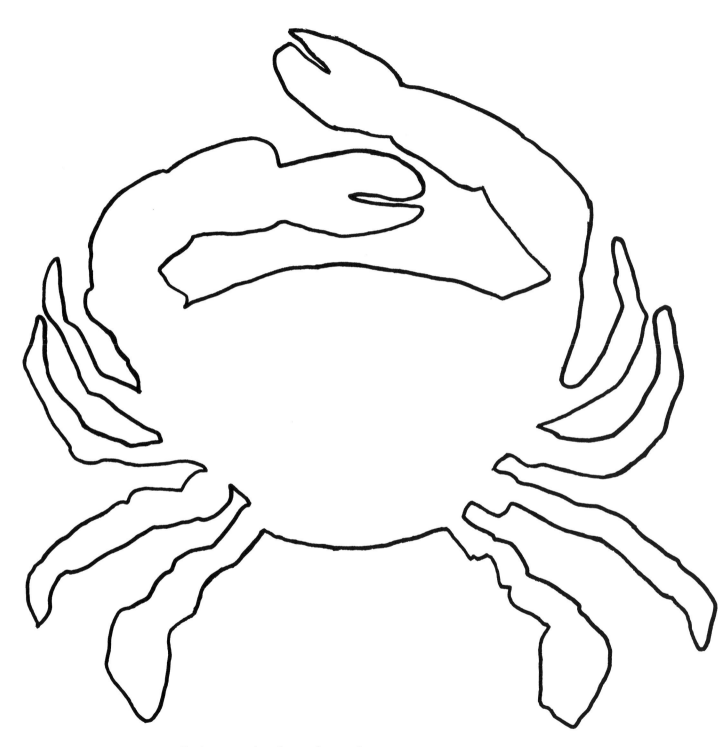

Crab image has been flopped to give correct orientation
when velvet crab is fused to brown fabric.

beside the binding formed by the last row of stitching to anchor the binding on the underside.

■ Bind the padded Front in the same way; there is no loop on the Front.

■ Joining the appliquéd Back and padded Front.

■ Pin the appliquéd Back to the padded Front, on their unbound sides, wrong sides together and raw edges matching, and machine stitch together. Then bind and finish the unbound edges as for the loop corner of the Back, allowing sufficient binding to cover the raw ends of the binding just completed and 10 mm (⅜ in) left unstitched at start and finish to turn under. Before folding binding over, finger press the turn-under to hide the raw edges of the ends.

Mitt with Plaiditude

The distinctive plaid which is the emblem
of the British fashion and luggage house
Burberrys has been put under the microscope
for this first-class oven mitt. The interlocking
threads of the warp and weft of the fabric are
expressed as knitting stitches and the resulting
pattern gives a greatly magnified impression
of the original. When finished, the knitting
was backed with a piece of felt, which is
wrapped around to the front and then held
fast with feather stitch worked in red.

INSTRUCTIONS

Materials

8-ply wool (50 g balls): one each of black, white, red and beige

pair of 4 mm knitting needles

wool sewing needle

craft square of black felt

key ring

Tension: 22 sts to 10 cm over stocking stitch, using 4 mm needles.

Finished size is 26.5 cm (10½ in) by 24 cm (9½ in) wide.

METHOD

■ Using 4 mm needles and black wook, cast on 56 sts.

■ Wind a small amount of red wool onto a bobbin or scrap of cardboard; little is used and the bobbin is less awkward to manage at the back of your work than a whole ball of wool.

■ Beginning with a knit row and referring to the graph for changes in colour, start the pattern.

■ Mitt is worked in stocking stitch, so every alternate row is purl.

■ When changing colours, carry the colour not in use across the wrong side (purl side) of the work. The build-up of wool will be covered by the felt backing and will act as insulating material for the mitt. Note, however, that the red vertical strip is confined to four stitches and does not need to 'travel' from side to side.

■ Cast off on the last row of pattern.

ADDING THE BACKING

■ With a cloth and steam iron, press the knitting flat then centre it, right side up, on the felt square.

■ Turn excess felt over onto the front of the mitt. Trim to leave a black felt 'frame' 2 cm (¾ in) wide. Mitre corners so that adjacent 'frame' sides meet at a neat 45° angle.

■ Pin hem and baste with black thread, making sure you catch in the felt at the back.

■ Unravel a length of red wool. Separate two of the plies and thread them into the wool needle. Decorate the strip of black felt at the front with feather stitch (see diagram).

■ Cover metal key ring with knotted black wool (see page 103 for diagram of knotted loop). Stitch wool-covered ring to one corner of mitt.

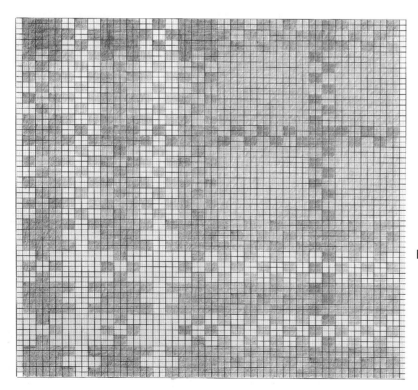

ONE SQUARE EQUALS ONE STITCH

FEATHER STITCH DIAGRAM

Mind Games

Whoever said knitting was a dull and repetitive task? Try your hand at the following pattern and you'll use those parts of your brain that are usually reserved for rocket science. What you end up with is a double-sided piece of fabric in black and white squares (so it can double as a chess or draughts board while the dinner cooks), but the squares are the opposite colour on the other side.

This is a variation on tubular knitting on two needles. You start knitting with black yarn only and slip every second stitch. On the following row, you knit only those stitches you previously slipped and slip the remainder. Thus two layers of fabric are worked at the same time, each with a purl and plain side. When the white is incorporated, there is much yarn forwarding and yarn backing, and then the real fun begins.

INSTRUCTIONS

Materials

12-ply wool: 50 g (2 oz) each of black and white

pair of 5.5 mm knitting needles

wool sewing needle

ring for holder

■ Using 5.5 mm needles and black wool (B), cast on 85 sts in K1, P1 rib, thus: make a sl knot and place it on left-hand needle (LHN), K1 into slip knot and place st on LHN, P1 through the 2 loops of this last st and sl onto LHN, *K1 through the 2 loops of last st and place on LHN, P1 through the 2 loops of last st and place on LHN; rep from *40 times more ... 85 sts.

■ 1st row: (yfwd, sl 1 purlwise, ybk, K1) 42 times, sl last st (slip knot) off needle and discard (for neatness, this would be an untidy looking stitch if left) ... 84 sts.

■ 2nd row: (yfwd, sl 1 purlwise, ybk, K1) 42 times.

■ Last 2 rows form 1 round of tubular stocking stitch.

■ Begin check pattern:

■ 3rd row: Yfwd, sl 1 purlwise, ybk, K1B, join in white wool (W), *(B & W yfwd, P1W, B & W ybk, K1B) 5 times, (B & W yfwd, P1B, B&W ybk, K1W), rep from * 3 times more, B & W yfwd, sl 1 purlwise, B ybk, K1B.

■ 4th row: B yfwd, sl 1 purlwise, B ybk, K1B, twist B & W to prevent gap *(B & W yfwd, P1W, B &W ybk, K1B) 5 times, (B & W yfwd, P1B, B &W ybk, K1W) 5 times; rep from * 3 times more, B & W yfwd, sl 1 purlwise, B ybk, K1B.

■ Rep 4th row 5 times more.

■ 10th row: B yfwd, sl 1 purlwise, B ybk, K1B, twist B & W to prevent gap *(B & W yfwd, P1B, B &W ybk, K1W) 5 times, (B & W yfwd, P1W, B &W ybk, K1B) 5 times; rep from * 3 times more, B & W yfwd, sl 1 purlwise, B ybk, K1B.

■ Rep 10th row 6 times more.

■ Work 4th row 7 times, then 10th row 7 times.

■ Continue in check pattern until there are 8 rows of checks in all.

■ Cut off W and, using B only, work 2nd row 4 times.

■ To cast off, cut B leaving 4 times the width of work and thread into wool sewing needle. Sl the sts alternately onto a pair of double-pointed knitting needles so the purl sts are on one needle and the knit stitches are on the other, then graft the two sets of sts together.

■ Cover metal key ring with knotted black wool (see page 103 for diagram of knotted loop) and stitch wool covered ring to one corner of mitt.

■ Abbreviations:See page 104.

Pretty Boy

The hand pockets at both ends of this double-ended oven mitt hinted at a birdcage shape and the budgie seemed a likely candidate.

Originally just one bird made as part of a string of toys to be stretched across the top of a crib or pram of a new baby, it was unpicked and divided perfectly in two. Then it was topstitched to a piece of fabric and filled, trapunto style, through a slash in the backing fabric.

To emphasise the 3-D effect, the line between the body and one wing was top-stitched, as were the wing and tail feather lines. The bird was cut out again and positioned on the pocket where it was topstitched again with the tail left free.

Patterns and directions are given for the bird, but for an effective shortcut, any small discarded soft toy could be divided in two and stitched to the mitt ends.

INSTRUCTIONS

Materials

tracing paper

1 m (1 yd) blue denim

20 cm x 40 cm (8 in x 16 in) light blue cotton

felt in yellow, green, light blue, white, brown and orange

fusible web

scrap of toy filling

two tiny black beads for eyes

pearl cotton in mid blue, brown and green

monofilament thread

yellow and denim blue thread

wadding

■ On tracing paper, trace over and cut out pattern pieces.

■ Iron small pieces of fusible web onto white, pale blue, brown, green and orange felt.

■ Holding paper pattern over right side of felt, cut two of each of these little pieces, flopping the pattern for the second one and keeping the flopped ones separate.

■ Cut out 2 bodies from yellow felt and 4 wings from green felt (no fusible web needed), flopping and separating as before.

■Peel paper from back of white face and blue eye mask and, using steam iron, fuse to top of body using placement pattern as a guide. Then fuse cheek and chest details and beak and cere membrane above it to face. Fuse eye mask and eye white to eye mask.

■ Hand stitch black bead over eye white.

■ With monofilament thread in top of machine, and small straight stitch, topstitch right wing to body following placement pattern, then topstitch left side of body to right wing.

■ Lay the budgie over a piece of light blue fabric and topstitch with monofilament around head, wings and tail. Slash backing fabric and introduce toy filling to fill the body, wings and tail, stuffing the body much more than wings and tail. Close the slash with hand stitches.

■ Topstitch the feather lines on tail and wings, then topstitch again on seam at the left side of body.

■ For the claws, make 6 knotted loops (see page 103 for knotting technique) in brown pearl cotton.

■ With green pearl cotton, make a twisted cord at least 36 cm (14 in) long, cut it in two and thread one half through the claws and knot ends. Reserve other cord for other budgie.

■ Make another budgie facing the opposite direction with the flopped felt pieces and without claws.

CAGE POCKET (MAKE 2)

■ Cut a piece of pale blue fabric 17 cm x 20 cm (6½ in x 8 in). Measure and rule parallel lines about 18 mm (½ in) apart, parallel with the long sides.

■ With monofilament thread in the top of the machine and a very narrow zigzag stitch, stitch mid blue pearl cotton over the lines to suggest cage wires.

■ Centre budgies over cages and topstitch down with monofilament thread, leaving tails free and arranging green pearl cotton perches as in photograph.

PADDED STRIP

■ From denim, cut 2 pieces 17 cm x 74 cm (6½ in x 29 in).

■ From wadding, cut one piece the same measurement and 2 pieces 17 cm x 20 cm (6½ in x 8 in).

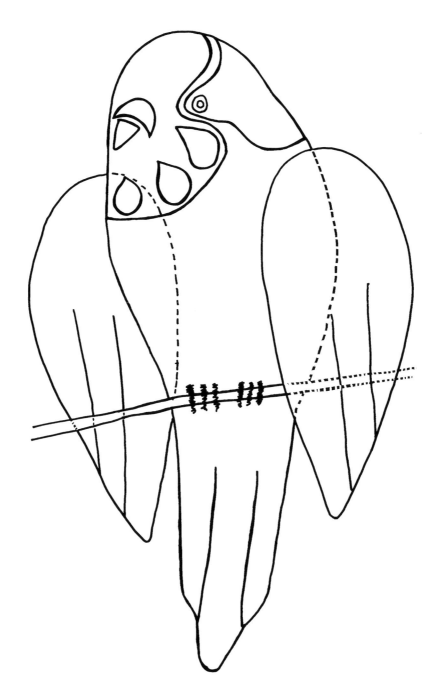

PLACEMENT & CUTTING PLAN

■ Sandwich the wadding between denim strips with wrong sides towards wadding and smaller wadding pieces at either end of the strip to form double layer of padding, and pin.

■ Thread machine with yellow thread and machine quilt through all layers in straight lines along and across the strip to form a chequered pattern.

ASSEMBLING MITT

■ Make bias binding — you will need around 2 m (2 ¼ yd) — and hanging loop following the directions on pages 28–31.

■ Bind the tail ends of both budgie pockets following directions as above.

■ Lay a budgie pocket over each end of strip with raw edges matching, and pin. Using scissors, round the corners.

■ Pin the loop in the middle of one edge on the other side of strip, raw edges matching. Then bind and finish as for Crab Claws mitt on pages 24–31.

Basket of Flowers

If you can't drag yourself away from the garden, bring it with you when kitchen duty calls. The pattern starts off in basket weave stitch (what else) and then the rim of the basket is knitted and joined back to the top of the basket weave. Stitches are divided for the handle and knitted in a single cable. The background is done last and joined to the handle with a flat seam.

Crocheted flowers were worked in tapestry wool, knitting cotton and knitting wool in order to obtain as much colour variation as possible. The crocheted chain stitch stems are stitched to the background, as is the grub with French knot eyes on the basket's rim.

INSTRUCTIONS

Materials

12-ply yarn, brown (B), sand (S) and green (G)

pair each of 6 mm and 5.5 mm knitting needles

one smaller-sized knitting needle

2 stitch holders

a cable needle

wool sewing needle

scraps of yarn in various blues, pinks and yellows for the flowers

crochet hook (preferably smaller than recommended size for

wool to achieve tight result)

lime green tapestry wool for the grub

bright red wool for grub's eyes

wadding

fusible web

calico (muslin)

12-ply yarn is used for the basket, which is made in one piece.

▨ Using 6 mm needles and B, cast on 32 sts (abbreviations on page 104).

1st row (right side): Knit.

2nd row: P1B, (K5S, P3B) 3 times, K5S, P2B.

3rd row: K2B, (P5S, K3B) 3 times, P5S, K1B.

4th row: As 2nd row.

5th row: Knit, using colours to match basket weave blocks.

6th row: K2S, (P3B, K5S) 3 times, P3B, K3S.

7th row: P3S, (K3B, P5S) 3 times, K3B, P2S.

8th row: As 6th row.

9th row: As 5th row.

Rep 2nd to 4th rows (12 rows in all).

13th row: Using B, knit inc in every st ... 64 sts.

■ Cont in rev st st (next row purl) for 7 rows.

■ Make hem. With wrong side facing, use smaller size knitting needle to pick up loops of first row of 64 sts then knit tog 1 st from each needle to end of row.

■ Divide for handle. K29, inc in each of next 3 sts , K1, inc in each of next 3 sts, turn.

■ Next row: P13, turn.

■ Cont on these 13 sts in cable patt for handle, leaving 29 stitches at beg and the 28 sts at end on stitch holders.

1st row (right side): P2, K9, P2.
2nd row: K2, P9, K2.
3rd row: P2, C6F, K3, P2.
4th row: As 2nd row.
Rep rows 1 and 2 once.
7th row: P2, K3, C6B, P2.
8th row: As row 2.
Rep last 8 rows 10 times more.
Dec row. K2tog 3 times, K1, K2tog 3 times ... 7 sts.

■ Join handle. Sl the first 4 sts and the last 3 sts onto spare needle, leaving 25 sts on each stitchholder. With a wool needle and B, use a flat seam to join side edges of basket. Graft the last 7 sts on spare needle to the end of the handle, taking care that handle is not twisted.

BACKGROUND

■ With right side facing, join G to first of 25 sts and using 5.5 mm needles, work 4 rows st st.

5th row: K2, M1, K to last 2 sts, M1, K1.
6th row: Purl.
Rep last 2 rows 3 times ... 33 sts.

Work a further 12 rows st st.

21st row: K1, sl 1, K1, psso, K to last 3 sts, K2tog, K1.

22nd row: Purl.

23rd row: As 21st row.

Work 4 rows st st.

Rep last 3 rows once.

31st row: As 21st row.

32nd row: P1, P2tog, P to last 3 sts, P2tog tbl, P1.

Rep last 2 rows 3 times … 11 sts.

Cast off.

■ Make other side the same.

■ Using a flat seam, join background to handle on each side.

■ Turn mitt inside out and place on a piece of wadding. Cut wadding the size of the background and another piece for the handle measuring 5 cm (2 in) by 47 cm (18½ in). Cut fusible web same size as wadding pieces.

■ With steam iron, press fusible web, paper side up, to wrong side of handle and wrong side of Front (which will have no flowers). Peel away paper and with pressing cloth and steam iron, fuse wadding to these same knitted pieces.

■ Cut a calico lining of two background shapes and a handle, adding seam allowances. Seam curved edge of each background piece to long side of handle, right sides together. Turn knitted mitt to right side, insert lining into mitt, wrong sides together, turn up a hem on lower edge of lining and slip stitch lining to inside of mitt.

FLOWERS

■ There are 18 blue and 19 pink flowers on this oven mitt.

■ Petals: Wind yarn three times around little finger, slip off, insert hook into resulting ring and fasten with a sl st. 1 ch and then dc into ring as many times as it takes to fill it tightly. Sl st into 1st ch. Fasten off, leaving a tail for attaching to background.

▨ Stems: With G and crochet hook, make crochet chains for stems in various lengths, leaving sufficient yarn when fastening off to stitch them to the background. I made 15 stems, which includes the one dangling over the basket's rim.

▨ Decide on an approximate arrangement of flowers in the basket, angle stems towards the proposed flowers and slip stitch in place with wool needle.

▨ Using tails left when fastening off, slip stitch each petal cluster in place. I decided I preferred their wrong sides being displayed.

▨ With yellow wool and wool needle, make hefty French knots in the centres of the flowers. Attach the dangling flower to its stem with French knots combined with slip stitch.

GRUB

▨ With lime green tapestry wool and 4 mm knitting needles, cast on 20 sts. Knit fours rows of garter stitch and cast off.

▨ Roll into a tight tube and, using wool needle, oversew with matching wool to fasten. Position on basket rim with a loop in the middle. Slip stitch to basket rim.

▨ Make red wool French knot eyes on both sides of one end.

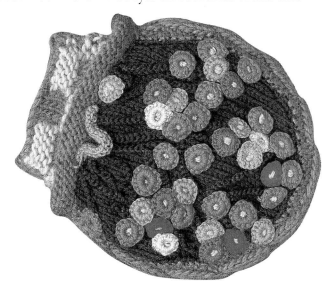

Hens in Safe Haven

The repeated image of a hen is not unknown in the world of craft, but the model for this hen oven mitt is in one of my favourite cookbooks, *Memories of Gascony* by Pierre Koffman, in a picture of the author's cousin beside a barn door, peeling garlic; the chooks are at her feet. My original plan was to work the hens in waste canvas, but the effect was coarse with overlarge stitches and too many gaps between them. They were worked instead over standard canvas tacked to the background; any visible canvas was snipped away when the needlepoint was finished. The chickens seemed a bit spread out, so I added a 'chicken wire' grid of grey knitting wool couched down with a tiny zigzag stitch in silver metallic thread. The 'links' are just dense bars of broad zigzag in the silver.

INSTRUCTIONS

Materials

woollen knitted fabric (cut-up jumper) for the three external pieces

tapestry wool in off-white, light tan, tan (2 skeins),

brown, crimson and light yellow

tapestry needle; fusible web

10 threads to the inch Penelope canvas; tweezers

small, sharp scissors

calico for backing the needlepoint

dark grey knitting wool

silver metallic sewing machine thread; lining fabric

thin (4 mm (⅛ in)) fusible wadding (batting)

string and wool for making knotted loop; wadding

■ Trace over and cut out pattern pieces for Coffee Pot mitt (pages 20–1). Note that this mitt has a more shovel-nosed top; this is to include more of the hen on the top left-hand side. Modify your pattern shape accordingly or repeat the images more densely.

■ Place Back pattern over the fabric intended for needlepoint hens, but do not cut out; draw around its outline with a marking pencil. Plot placement of hens so they are repeated regularly and within the confines of the mitt. Do vertical alignments through the legs and horizontals through heads and tails.

■ Cut canvas into six 10-cm (4-in) squares. Bind edges with masking tape to prevent fraying and mark centre points of squares. Find centre of hen (marked by arrows and dot on graph), centre one canvas square on this point and tack to fabric.

■ Count threads from the centre to your starting point (or start in the centre) and work hen in tent stitch, referring to the graph for colour changes. Note that the beak is worked in a tent stitch going the opposite direction. Complete remaining hens in this way, working on the portions within the mitt on the top right-hand and bottom left-hand corners.

■ When finished, clip away canvas from outer stitches with small, sharp scissors. Then carefully extract threads from the edge of the work with tweezers and scissors. Canvas beneath the centre of the hens cannot be seen.

■ With a steam iron, fuse web to calico. Peel away paper and press to wrong side of hens.

■ Thread top of sewing machine with silver thread. Draw diagonal lines at 5.5 cm (2¼ in) intervals with ruler and marking pencil over the hens. Couch down grey knitting wool over drawn lines with a tiny zigzag stitch to suggest chicken wire.

■ Change stitch setting to wide, dense zigzag and stitch junctions of chicken wire.

■ Stack and sew the mitt pieces in the sequence recommended for the Coffee Pot mitt on page 19. Finish the bottom edge and make a knotted loop according to these same instructions.

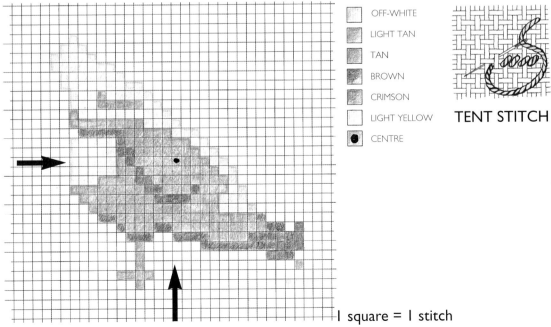

OFF-WHITE

LIGHT TAN

TAN

BROWN

CRIMSON

LIGHT YELLOW

CENTRE

TENT STITCH

I square = I stitch

Still Life with Tulips

Appliqué has a rich and venerable past, with many different cultures and civilisations employing the technique for domestic furnishings, heraldry, livery and religious vestments. Appliqué is at its best when shapes are simple and colours are carefully combined; it is well known that the intuitive selection of suitable fabrics lies at the core this craft's success. As well as the repeated patterns and symbols for which appliqué is famous, there is another side to the technique — picture building, where balance and composition partner shape and colour. Start with a background and upon this build a composition around a central image.

The starting point for this mitt was a piece of lipstick pink heavy furnishing chintz. Tulip images came from two quite different furnishing fabrics and are in a tea-dyed ticking jug with grosgrain ribbon handle. The stalks are a type of cord with the intriguing name of rat-tail. Outer ring of the tabletop is pale with a darker centre section, and over both is a subtly printed furnishing voile. The winged insect in the lower left corner adds a traditional Dutch master touch which goes perfectly with the tulips.

INSTRUCTIONS

Materials

25 cm (10 in) square lipstick pink chintz for appliqué background

fabric scraps of flower prints from which to cut six blooms

at least 6 to 7 cm (2½ to 3 in) long

calico (muslin) scraps

14 cm (5½ in) of 13 mm (½ in) wide cream grosgrain ribbon for handle

45 cm (½ yd) gold rat tail cord

scrap of heavy cotton drill in cream

scrap of mattress ticking dyed in tea

scrap of cream furnishing voile with sprig print

fabric scap printed with small winged insect

cream, gold, red and mid tan thread

permanent black marking pen

1 m (1 yd) black poplin for lining and binding

thin (4 mm (⅛ in)) fusible wadding (batting)

fusible web

wadding (batting)

APPLIQUÉ

■ Cut out flowers roughly and back them with pieces of fusible wadding.

■ Build the appliqué from the bottom layer up, starting with the background. Mark the curved corners of the finished mitt in dressmaker's pencil to ensure the design fits comfortably. Cut a curved piece of drill for the table in the left-hand corner using the photograph as a guide, back it with fusible web, peel away paper and iron it to the chintz.

■ Fuse a 3.5-cm (1¼-in) strip of calico to this edge. Over this fuse voile cut to the full table shape. Stitch around this edge with a dense, broad machine buttonhole stitch.

■ Trace over jug diagram (see page 102) and cut out a pattern. From ticking, cut a base and fusible web, remembering to cut it with the rough (fusing) side up. Repeat on the drill for top of jug and calico for jug interior. Cut a strip of web to match the ribbon.

■ Iron web to wrong side of jug pieces and ribbon. Peel away paper from backs of ribbon and fabric pieces and 'assemble' jug on the table, using photograph as a placement guide. Mitre ribbon corner and tuck ends under base and side before ironing pieces in place. Stitch around jug as for table.

■ Decide on flower placement in order to plot the path of the stems. Butt the stems against the near rim of jug and attach to background with zigzag stitch in gold thread.

■ Trim flowers to their finished shape, pin in place at tops of stems and stitch down with straight stitch and matching thread. Edge them with dense buttonhole stitch in red or mid tan.

■ Cut out the winged insect, back it with fusible web and iron to lower left-hand corner. Stitch around it with straight stitch to anchor, then edge with a narrow buttonhole stitch in mid tan. Draw on antennae and legs with permanent marking pen.

■ Finish the oven mitt following the instructions for Crab Claws on page 29, using the poplin for the front of the padded section, linings, bindings and loop, and hang it with pride in your kitchen.

Pig Portrait

It was the hairiness of white pigs which suggested to me the use of towelling in this farmyard portrait. The pig pictured on a page of wonderful pork and rabbit recipes in *France: A Culinary Journey* (Angus & Robertson) seemed to beg for interpretation in another medium. I eliminated some of the elements of the composition to make it a workable appliqué.

Layering the face and the forehead/muzzle throws these sections into relief and promotes a three-dimensional look. Emphasis is given to the various planes of the face and body by topstitching outlines with monofilament to make 'valleys' in the pile of the towelling.

The snout required pale pink cotton knit. Having none at the critical moment, I cut into an old T-shirt and dyed it pink with food colouring.

The eye colour was another stumbling block. Even pig owners were vague about the subject. Everyone who would have known at the pork research board was at a conference when I phoned. I made them the same colour as the trotters; a kind of grey-brown worked in satin stitch with the needle threaded with grey and brown. A steely blue-grey, the colour of lead, was the later reply from a pig owner who did first-hand research.

INSTRUCTIONS

Materials

Towelling in pink, light pink and black

(new or used face washers are suitable)

scrap of knitting

hessian (burlap)

scraps of brown and grey fabric (for trotters), fawn drill,

apricot cotton, pink fine knit cotton

25 cm x 50 cm (10 in x 20 in) pink fabric for lining

scrap of toy filling

fusible web

monofilament thread

grey and brown stranded embroidery thread

wadding (batting)

1.4 m (1½ yd) home made black bias binding with fusible

web attached (see page 28 for cutting and method)

string

APPLIQUÉ

■ Trace over diagram and join in right leg. Note that diagram is for placement of appliqué as well as for pattern pieces, and that the pattern pieces have to be flopped in order to cut out fusible web on paper side.

■ Cut black towelling background 25 cm (10 in) square.

■ From light pink towelling, cut one piece shaped around the top of head incorporating ears and back.

■ From pink towelling, cut one piece incorporating front legs, face and side. Also from pink towelling, cut one piece for the face and another for the forehead and muzzle.

■ Using the photograph as a guide, cut hessian for wall on right, drill for the triangular shadow between right leg and snout, and knitting for the wall on left.

■ From brown and grey scraps, cut trotters. Cut inner ears from apricot cotton.

■ Flop all patterns for all the above pieces and cut out fusible web on paper side. Bond web to undersides of fabric pieces.

■Remove paper and bond fabric pieces with steam iron to background in following order, using photograph as a placement guide. Hessian wall, triangular shadow, pale pink head top, largest pink piece, face, forehead/muzzle, inner ears, knitted wall and trotters.

■Cut two 5 cm (2½ in) circles from fine cotton knit. Stitch together around outside, leaving gap for turning. Turn, fill with toy filling, close gap with slip stitches. Manipulate the padded snout until it is the right size and thickness, pulling excess knit fabric to the rear and fastening with hand tacking. Hand stitch from side to side through centre for snout division. Hand stitch a row of running stitches around top half of snout's circumference close to the edge to make a ridge. On either side of the center of snout division, hand stitch from front to back, pulling firmly on thread to make nostrils.

■ Thread top of machine with monofilament thread and, using small zigzag stitch, anchor all pieces.

■ Stitch over the design lines shown on the diagram to make orbits above eyes and all other outlines.

■ Thread sewing needle with a strand each of brown and grey thread and satin stitch the eyes.

■ Hand stitch snout to the muzzle.

■ Finish mitt as for Crab Claws (see pages 24—31), using the pink fabric for lining and black towelling for the right side of the padded Front. Instead of a bias binding loop, make a knotted loop around a loop of string following directions on page 103 with wool to match the knitted scrap.

PLACEMENT AND
PATTERN PIECE DIAGRAM
When tracing, join in right leg.

Major Mittchell

Rich gold sunflowers and sulphur-crested cockatoos were the inspirations for this mitt, which combines a knit pattern with the frivolity of crochet for the cockatoo and his bright yellow comb.

Although this mitt can be made entirely in knitting yarn, you may wish to use tapestry wool for brighter colours, rather than the sunburnt tones of the Australian bush. You can also play around with the textures — different types of thread, a cockatoo in felt with a comb in wool. The only limit is your imagination … and the materials at hand.

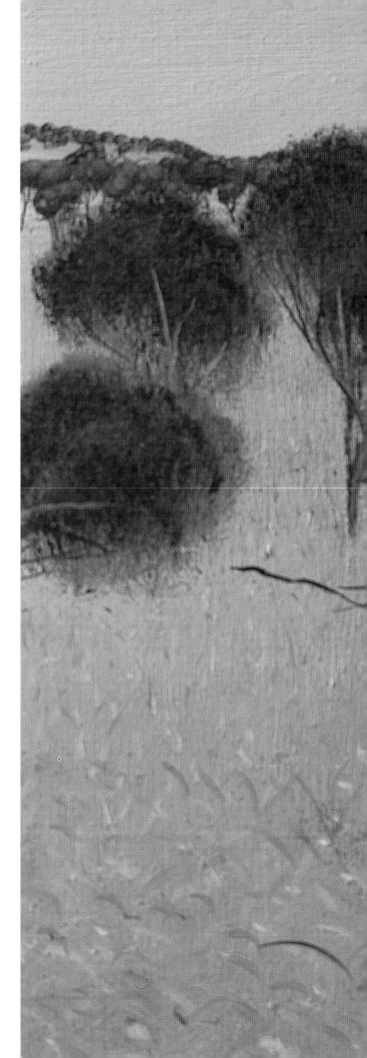

INSTRUCTIONS

Materials

black 12-ply wool 100g

6 mm knitting needles; small amount of green 12-ply wool

small amounts of fine white, grey, yellow, dark brown, lighter

brown, orange, green and black wool OR felt in same colours

fine crochet hook, about 2 mm

wool sewing needle; lining fabric;

wadding (batting); metal ring

MITT

▨ Using 6 mm needles and 12-ply wool, cast on 51 sts.

Work 6 rows stocking stitch (st st).

Shape thumb. 1st row: K23, M1, K5, M1, K23.

Work 3 rows st st.

5th row: K23, M1, K7, M1, K23.

Work 3 rows st st.

9th row: K23, M1, K9, M1, K23.

▨ Cont in this way, inc as before in foll 4th rows until there are 63 sts.

Thumb. 1st row: K40, turn.

2nd row: P17, turn.

3rd row: Cast on 2 sts, knit to end ... 19 sts.

Work 11 rows st st.

Shape top. 1st row: K1, (K2tog, K1) to end.

2nd row: Purl.

▨ Rep last 2 rows once, break off wool and run through rem 9 sts, fasten securely and, using a flat seam, join sides of thumb.

▨ With right side facing, use right-hand needle to knit up 2 sts from cast-on sts at base of thumb; knit across rem 23 sts on left-hand needle ... 48 sts.

■ Cont in st st for 9 cm.

■ Shape top. 1st row: K1, K2tog, K18, sl1, K1, psso, K2, K2tog, K18, sl1, K1, psso, K1.
2nd and alt rows: Purl.
3rd row: K1, K2tog, K16, sl1, K1, psso, K2, K2tog, K16, sl1, K1, psso, K1.
5th row: K1, K2tog, K14, sl1, K1, psso, K2, K2tog, K14, sl1, k1, psso, K1.
7th row: K1, K2tog, K12, sl1, K1, psso, K2, K2tog, K12, sl1, K1, psso, K1.
8th row: P1, P2tog, P10, P2tog tbl, P2, P2tog, P10, P2tog tbl, P1.
Cast off.

■ Using flat seam, join sides of mitt together.

■ If working the decorative pieces in crochet, use the full-size diagram as an aid to shaping them. Alternatively, cut some or all parts from felt and appliqué in place.

STEM

■ Using 12-ply green wool and 6 mm knitting needles, cast on sufficient sts for length of stem.

■ Work in stocking stitch for about 2.5 cm.

■ Cast off.

■ Allow stem to roll together with reverse st st side showing and stitch cast-on and cast-off edges together.

■ Work another stem of appropriate length in the same way.

LEAF

■ Using fine green wool and crochet hook, make a chain the length of A to B on leaf diagram. 1dc in each ch from B to A. 3 dc in last ch at A. 1dc in each ch along other side from A to B.

■ Next row. 1dc in each dc, inc at curve as necessary to keep work flat, end at C.

■ Rep last row, ending in turn at D, E, F, G and H. Fasten off.

FLOWER

■ Using dark brown wool and crochet hook, work a circle in rounds of dc to match the inner circle of diagram of flower centre.

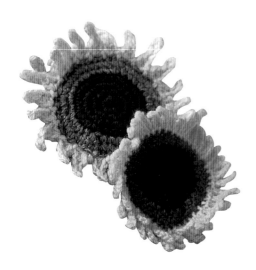

■ Join in lighter brown wool and work one or two more rounds of dc to finish centre.

■ For petals, join yellow wool to dc on edge of centre, *work chain for about 2.5 cm, sl st in each ch, 1dc in next dc of centre.

■ Rep from * around centre, sl st in first ch at beg.

■ Fasten off. Work two more flowers to match diagram.

COCKATOO

■ Using white wool, make a number of chain the length of neck edge.
1st row: 1dc in each ch to end.
2nd row: 1ch 1dc in each dc to end.

■ Rep last row, shaping work to match shape of cockatoo on diagram, work htr and tr and short rows to extend the top front of head.

■ From point X, make a number of chain the length of the first white feather of the crest, sl st in each ch, changing to dc, htr and tr to shape the feather. Sl st in next st in top of head.

■ Join yellow wool to tip of white feather, make a number of chain the length of yellow part of feather, sl st in each ch, then work dc, htr and tr in white sts to base of feather.

■ Sl st in next st in top of head.

■ Using yellow, make three more feathers across the top of head the same way as the first white feather. Work length of of chain as indicated in the diagram. Fasten off.

■ For eye, use fine white wool to work a small circle in dc. Fasten off and stitch to head.

■ Using black wool, work a French knot for the pupil.

■ For beak, with wrong side facing, join grey wool to side of head and work a row of dc into ends of head rows.

■ Next row. Work dc, htr and tr to form beak shape. Add further rows if required to match diagram shape.

■ Fasten off. A piece of grey felt cut to shape may be easier.

■ To assemble, arrange the pieces as shown in the diagram and hand stitch in place with matching wool.

■ Use the mitt to draw a pattern for the lining. Trim 2 cm from the wrist edge to allow for the hem.

■ Use the pattern to cut one piece from wadding. Cut one lining piece, adding a seam allowance to all edges except the wrist edge.

■ Turn the mitt inside out and place the wadding on the palm. Position the lining on top, turn the edges of the lining under the wadding and hand stitch in place. Turn up hem on wrist edge and stitch.

■ Knot black wool over ring to cover, see knottted loop method on page 103. Using end of wool, stitch ring to corner of mitt.

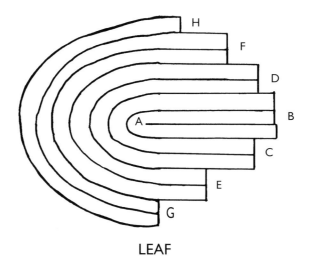

LEAF

COCKY'S THUMB OUTLINE
JOINS OUTLINE ON OPPOSITE PAGE
ALONG DOTTED LINE

— X

COCKY'S OUTLINE

Mitt-a-Leekie

Leeks are lovely; decorative as well as delicious. Although the current vogue is for tiny vegetables, a large leek was the model for this appliqué.

Hessian on the bias gives a good, earthy kind of background. The leaves were cut from self-patterned furnishing fabrics in two different greens, the bulb is calico and lining is a plain green fabric. To suggest roots, I anchored lots of short lengths of kitchen string beneath the bulb, covered their ends with three strands of the same string and held it all in place with machine zigzag. The white part of the leek is outlined in a single row of string.

Parallel(ish) lines of machine stitching in light green do a good impersonation of leaf veins and the leaves are outlined in dense buttonhole stitch.

INSTRUCTIONS

Materials

60 cm (⅔ yd) of natural hessian

2 different fabric pieces 20 cm x 25 cm (8 in x 10 in)

for Palm / Thumb and Front

20 cm (¼ yd) of 90 cm (36 in) green lining fabric

fusible web

thin (4 mm (⅛ in)) fusible wadding (batting)

wadding (batting)

cream kitchen string

monofilament thread

light green, mid green, darker green

and cream thread

natural string for a knotted loop

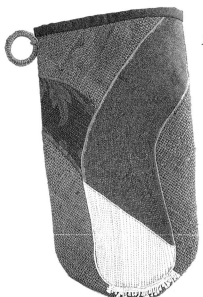

■ The basic pattern and method for this mitt are the same as the Coffee Pot mitt on pages 14–23, but the appliqué is simpler.

■ From the hessian fabric, cut one Back on the bias and Palm / Thumb and Front from designated fabrics on straight grain. Cut Palm / Thumb and Front from wadding, linings from all three pattern pieces and Back from fusible wadding.

■ Trace over leek diagram and cut out. Using traced patterns, cut leaves and bulb in fabrics, flop patterns and cut fusible web pieces. Fuse web to wrong side of fabrics.

■ Attach the fusible wadding to the wrong side of the Back, then position the leek motif on the Back and steam press in place.

■ Edge the whole calico bulb part with kitchen string and anchor with small zigzag and matching thread.

■ Press a very narrow strip of fusible web to the baseline of leek. Remove paper.

■ Cut about thirty 10-mm (⅜-in) lengths of string and place them over the strip of web and press gently with steam iron. Cover bulb ends of string 'roots' with 3 rows of string and fasten with small cream zigzag stitch.

■ Thread machine with mid green and stitch parallel lines to suggest veins on bulb and leaves.

■ Change thread to light green and work both sides of larger leaf in wide, dense buttonhole. Thread machine with mid green and work over both sides of smaller leaf in dense buttonhole.

■ Stack and sew the mitt pieces in the sequence recommended for the Coffee Pot on page 19.

FINISHING THE LOWER EDGE

■ Cut a 5-cm (2-in) wide strip of lining fabric long enough to fit around the base of the oven mitt, adding seam allowances to both short ends. Back it with a same size strip of fusible wadding.

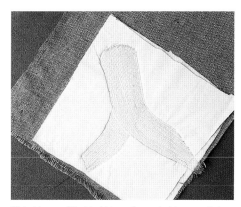

■ **1.** Use up filled bobbins when stitching parallel lines; bobbin doesn't have to match needle thread.

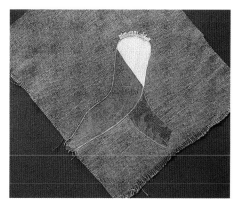

■ **2.** Completed appliqué before making mitt.

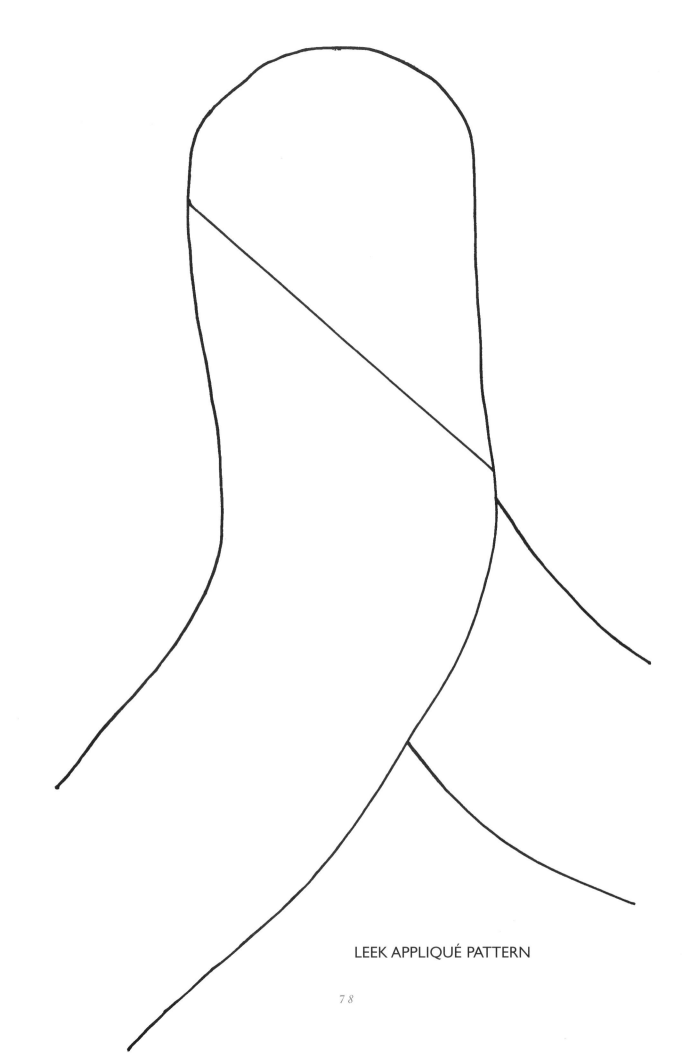

LEEK APPLIQUÉ PATTERN

■ With wrong sides together, seam short ends together to form a loop. Press seam open.

■ Fit loop over base of oven mitt, right sides together, seam in centre of oven mitt front and raw edges matching. Join with a 10-mm (⅜-in) straight stitch seam.

■ Fold up a 10-mm (⅜-in) hem on the raw edge and pin it to just over the line of stitching from the previous seam on the inside of the mitt. Stitch through from the right side in the crevasse made by the last seam to catch in the hem on the inside.

■ Make a string knotted loop over a circle of string (see diagram on page 103) and hand stitch it to the side seam of base for hanging.

Tally-ho

It is surely a little eccentric to make a needlepoint oven mitt, but I couldn't resist the foxes in Elizabeth Bradley's glorious book *Decorative Victorian Needlework*, published by Guild Publishing. The author explains how the Victorians put strange things in their needlework patterns; stranger still to include them on an oven mitt. But it was very enjoyable and I did make modifications for the rough nature of the item.

Instead of proper needlework canvas, I used hessian, partly because it inexpensive, I already had some and it is nice and floppy in the hand; not stiff like canvas. I also had some smoky blue 8-ply knitting wool, not really enough to make anything substantial, but sufficient for the background. The cross stitches of the fox heads are worked in tapestry wool, but because it was 'just an oven mitt' I decided to make them over two intersecting threads instead of one. Where the hessian thread peeped through, I trammed beneath the stitches with the same colour to add bulk.

The great success was the knitting wool, worked over one stitch; the area was covered quickly with diagonal tent stitch which also stops the work from distorting into a diamond shape.

INSTRUCTIONS

Materials

30 cm x 40 cm (12 in x 14 in) piece of hessian

tapestry wool: off white, dark brown (2),

red brown (2), ginger (2)

50 g (2 oz) of 8-ply wool in smoky blue

20 cm (¼ yd) of 90 cm (36 in) wide navy fabric

25 cm (¼ yd) of 90 cm (36 in) lining fabric

wadding (batting)

navy thread

wool and string for a knotted loop

■ Mitt is the same shape and construction as Coffee Pot on pags 14–23, but the Back is cut on the straight grain of the fabric.

■ Trace and cut pattern for the Back, centre the pattern piece over the hessian and draw around it with a dressmaker's pencil. Work the foxes and background within this shape. Find centre of Back and mark it with a ruled dressmaker's pencil line. Place the centre line of the centre fox's muzzle on this line. Note that chin line of side foxes is in line with the second last stitch of the centre foxes. Plot your arrangement of fox heads so that the lower ones do not disappear into the hem.

■ Following graph, work in cross stitch over two intersecting threads of hessian. Do not pull wool too tight or hessian threads will be revealed.

■ When foxes are complete, change to knitting yarn and fill in background with diagonal tent stitch (see page 103 for tent stitch), working downwards diagonally from left to right, forming vertical stitches on the back. On the return journey upwards from right to left, the stitches at the front slot in between the stitches of the previous row.

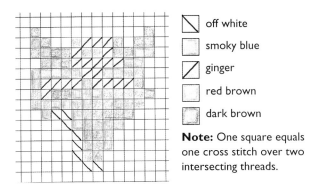

off white

smoky blue

ginger

red brown

dark brown

Note: One square equals one cross stitch over two intersecting threads.

Horizontal stitches are formed at the back, which interlock with those of the previous row and form a basketweave grid. The resulting fabric is very dense and sturdy.

■ When finished, cut out Back using and all the other pieces needed for construction and follow the directions on page 19 to complete the mitt.

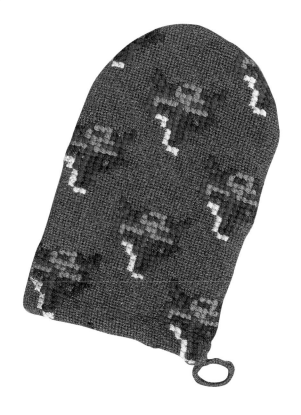

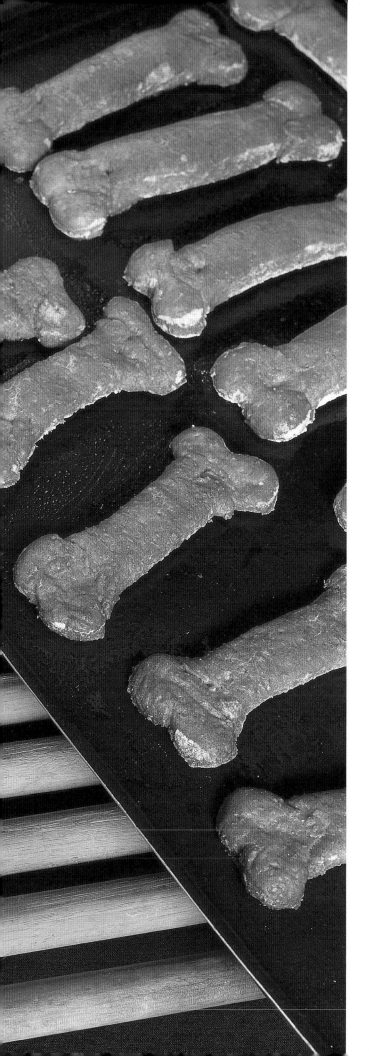

Dog's Dinner

Dogs always appreciate a little bit of worship from humans. Show them you care by making a striped oven mitt with repeat patterns in knitting stitch of man's best friend.

Originally a cross stitch design on a bookmark in Jana Houschild Linberg's *Cross Stitch Animals* (Cassell), the knitted version changes the shape of the dog to a more low-slung breed because knitted stitches aren't square; they are wider than they are long.

The result is a kind of cairn terrier with a chihuahua's tail. A stitch added or subracted to the design will change the breed accordingly.

INSTRUCTIONS

Materials

8-ply wool: 50 g (2 oz) each of white (W) and grey (G)

pair of 4 mm needles

wool sewing needle

lining fabric

wadding (batting)

metal ring

▩ Knitted in one piece in stripes; dogs embroidered in knitting stitch.

GLOVE

▩ Using 4 mm needles and G, cast on 80 sts (abbreviations on page 104).

Beginning with a knit row, work 7 rows st st.

Change to W and work 7 rows st st, inc at each end of 2nd row. Cont in st st in stripes of 7 rows G and 7 rows W, inc at each end of next and every following 6th row until there are 100 sts.

Work another stripe (7 rows) of W and 6 more rows of G.

Shape thumb: Keeping stripes correct as before, K14, turn.

Next row: Purl.

Cont on these 14 sts, dec at each end of next and foll alt rows

4 times ... 6 sts.

Work 1 row.

Cast off.

▩ Shape fingers: Keeping stripes correct as before, with right side facing, join wool to next st, K72, turn.

Next row. Purl.

Cont on these 72 sts, dec at each end of next and foll alt rows

4 times ... 64 sts.

Work 1 row.

Next row: Sl 1, K1, psso, K28, K2tog, sl 1, K1, psso, K28, K2tog.

Next and alt rows: Purl.

Next row: Sl 1, K1, psso, K26, K2tog, sl 1, K1, psso, K26, K2tog.

Cont in this way, dec in alt rows until 24 sts rem.

Work 1 row.

Cast off.

■ Shape Thumb: Keeping stripes correct as before, with right side facing, join wool to next st and knit to end … 14 sts.

■ Work as for other Thumb.

■ Follow graph (see page 103) to work dogs in knitting stitch.

■ Use the completed knitting to draw a pattern of the glove ending wrist edge level with the beginning of the first white stripe. Use pattern to cut one each from lining and wadding., adding a small seam allowance to all but wrist edge. Pin wadding to wrong side of lining and machine stitch seam, with right sides together. Use a flat seam to join knitted piece around thumb and fingers. Slip lining into glove. Turn up hem of first grey stripe to cover raw edge of lining and hand stitch in place.

■ Knot grey wool over ring to cover ring (see knotted loop method on page 103) and stitch with matching wool to a corner.

Fabergé in the Kitchen

In John Booth's book *The Art of Fabergé* (Bloomsbury), there is magic on every page, but it was the photograph of Tsar Nicholas II's gold and jewelled cigarette case that seemed destined for reinterpretation on an oven mitt.

Made by workmaster Henrik Wigström, it is a diamond-bordered aerial view of the Tsar's favourite resort in the Crimea. The Black Sea is set with calibré-cut sapphires and the mountains are textured gold. A line of calibré-cut rubies marks the road from Sebastopol to Yalta, with precious stones for towns and the railway is a line of emeralds.

Although the mitt version has a sturdy work-a-day side for handling hot pots and pans, it remains a special occasion piece with auction-house potential.

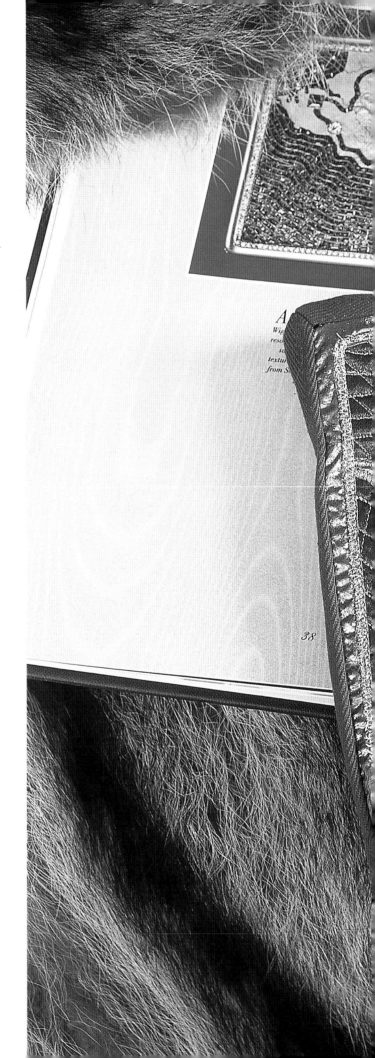

INSTRUCTIONS

Materials

28 cm (11 in) of denim, gold lamé, and metallic blue fabric

30 cm (12 in) of 4-mm (⅛-in) wide satin

ribbon in red and green

pearl cotton in lighter red and green

90 cm (1 yd) of 4-mm (⅛-in) wide gold

and silver ribbon (diamond border)

6 stitch-on jewels

gold metallic thread

blue, red and green thread

thin (4 mm (⅛ in)) fusible wadding (batting)

wadding (batting)

1.5 m (1⅝ yd) heavy woven cotton tape 6 cm (2½ in) wide

■ Finished size is about 24 cm (9½ in) square for padded side with the back of hand decorated side measuring the same width, but 20 cm (8 in) from top to bottom.

■ Note: Use low heat settings on iron and pressing cloth when bonding lamé and metallic fabrics to fusible web.

■ Bond fusible web to back of lamé piece measuring 28 cm x 24 cm (11 in x 9½ in).

■ Trace over diagram to make two pattern pieces for the Black Sea. Cut both pieces from metallic blue fabric.

■ Position Black Sea fabric on gold lamé, pin in place and stitch down with straight stitch close to edges.

■ Thread machine with gold metallic thread and cover edge of shoreline with wide dense buttonhole stitch.

▓ Thread machine with blue thread and stitch lines across the sea at right angles to the shore on both pieces.

▓ With gold thread, stitch lines parallel to shore, following diagram if desired. (These lines can be stitched with free motion machine embroidery. See method in Crab Claws, pages 26–7). Stitch lines two or three times more for definition.

▓ Turn steam iron to medium setting, hold it just above lamé mountain fabric and steam until the surface buckles. With gold metallic thread, stitch in minor roads on the land.

▓ Referring to diagram, plot the course of the road and railway and pin down, mitring ribbon to turn corners. Stitch down ribbon by machine with matching thread.

▓ With needle threaded with pearl cotton to match ribbon and starting at the right, draw needle up on one side of the ribbon and insert it directly opposite on the other side. Then bring it up again 4 mm (⅛ in) further along the ribbon. Continue, making a pattern of short stitches at right angles to the long sides.

▓ Cover outer edges of Black Sea with silver and gold tape and stitch down on both long sides with gold thread.

▓ Measure and cut four lengths of blue tape to frame decorative work. Machine each side on separately, right sides together, allowing 1 cm (⅜ in) between stitching line and Black Sea. Mitre corners, trim excess tape from corners and press flat.

■ From denim, cut a lining for the decorative Back and seam to lower edge of tape frame, right sides together, to give a 13 mm (½ in) depth of frame. Stitch, fold back to right way and press so seam is at edge.

■ Sandwich wadding between two 25-cm (10-in) squares of denim. Quilt through all layers in a diamond pattern, with stitching lines 4 cm (1⅝ in) apart.

■ Cut a Front lining from denim same size as padding.

JOINING PADDED FRONT TO DECORATIVE BACK

■ Stack pieces in this order from the bottom up with tops together — padded Front, right side up; decorative Back, lining side up; lining for Front, wrong side up. Stitch around 3 sides, leaving bottom open. Turn through to right way.

LOOP

■ Cut a 15-cm (6-in) length of tape and fold in edges on long sides, then fold again so the first folds meet; stitch close to the edge. Cross over ends and lay at right side centre of padded Front's bottom edge, raw edges matching. Place tape cut the length of the bottom plus end hems over this, right sides together and seam, catching in loop. Turn to right side, fold in ends and long edge of tape and pin to lining of padded Front. Hand stitch to close tape binding.

■ To finish, stitch on jewels to represent towns.

CUTTING AND STITCHING DIAGRAM FOR FABERGÉ IN THE KITCHEN

Naming Rights

It's a simple idea, but highly effective — an enclosure for a hot handle of a frying pan or skillet. I picked apart a model made and sold especially for the Le Creuset brand of cookware. I wasn't quite sure if the loop at the side, an extension of the bias binding, was a tab for the thumb or a hanger. Anyway, if they are thumb tabs, I put one on each side so the holder is equally suited to left-handers.

I made this one from grey towelling, with a plaid pattern of strips of my daughter's woven name tags, a legacy of her long-since-gone school days. It is destined for my daughter's kitchen for her Le Creuset frying pan.

INSTRUCTIONS

Materials

towelling and canvas measuring 16 cm x 15 cm (6¼ in x 6 in)

90 cm (1 yd) bias strip 4.5 cm (1¾ in) wide

name tags stitched into strips

monofilament

red thread

■ Place towelling over canvas, pin and stitch diagonally to quilt with stitching lines spaced 3.5 cm (1½ in) apart. (Holder will be folded in two on the shorter sides.)

■ Place name tag strips over quilting lines and weave them over and under each other. Stitch down on both edges with monofilament.

■ Change to red thread and add rows of dense buttonhole stitch between the strips of tags.

■ Press in hem edges of bias strip on long sides, and then press again so the folded edges meet. Pin and stitch bias binding to one short edge.

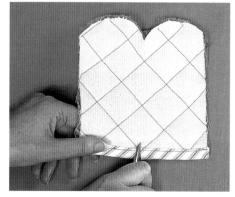

■ **1.** Using sharp scissors, carefully snip through the bias and towelling/canvas layers to a depth of around 1.5 cm (⅝ in).

■ **2.** The tabs on either side of the handle-holder can be used either for hanging the holder when not in use or, as seen here, as a thumb tab for either left- or right-handers.

Using scissors, snip through the bias and towelling/canvas to a depth of 1.5 cm (⅝ in). Fold at this mark to make two sides and press. Round the top corners with scissors.

■ Centre binding at midpoint of rounded corner and pin down both sides to the previously bound edge. Tack binding in place.

■ Thumb tabs need only be 10 cm (4 in) long. Trim and stitch folded edges of thumb tabs. Bend tabs back to the same side and tuck in ends, sewn edge 5 cm (2 in) from corner.

■ Stitch binding in place from thumb tab side, catching in edges of thumb tabs as you go.

Souvenir d'Afrique

Cast-off meets exotica in this exceptional oven mitt. The underside is cut from a pilled woollen jumper and the top is a precious scrap of Warner furnishing chintz; cutting into it was an exercise in courage, but at least now it can be displayed, used and enjoyed instead of hiding its splendour in a dark cupboard. The *Giraffa camelopardalis* and the two berobed attendants fitted quite nicely on the back of the glove-style mitt.

The 'dark continent' has always intrigued Europeans and, in the first half of the 1800s, the first giraffe arrived in Paris to wide acclaim. So great was the interest in the tallest mammal that household wares, clothing and knick knacks were produced reflecting this obsession and this fabric has its design history in this period.

INSTRUCTIONS

Materials

20 cm (¼ yd) of printed fabric

discarded woollen garment or 20 cm (¼ yd) of fabric

20 cm (¼ yd) of 90 cm (36 in) calico (muslin)

thin (4 mm (⅛ in)) fusible wadding (batting)

wadding (batting)

brown thread

small black bead for eye

scrap of knitting wool for a knotted loop

■ The basic pattern and method for this mitt are the same as the Coffee Pot mitt on pages 14–23, however the Back (printed fabric) is cut on the straight grain of the fabric, and there is no appliqué here.

■ After cutting out all the pieces, attach the fusible wadding to the wrong side of the Back. Thread the machine with brown thread and, with a small straight stitch, stitch around the outside of major images on the printed fabric (giraffe, reins, attendants, shoreline in this instance).

■ Stack and sew the mitt pieces in the sequence recommended on page 19.

FINISHING THE LOWER EDGE

■ Cut a 10-cm (4-in) wide strip of printed fabric long enough to fit around the base of the oven mitt, adding seam allowances to both short ends. Back it with a same size strip of fusible wadding.

■ With wrong sides together, seam short ends together to form a loop. Press seam open.

■ Fit loop over base of oven mitt, right sides together, seam in centre of oven mitt front and raw edges matching. Join with a 10-mm (⅜-in) straight stitch seam.

■ Fold up a 10-mm (⅜-in) hem on the raw edge and pin it to just over the line of stitching from the previous seam on the inside of the mitt. Stitch through from the right side in the crevasse made by the last stitch to catch in the hem on the inside.

■ Hand stitch the bead over the eye.

■ Make a woollen knotted loop over a circle of wool (see diagram on page 103) and hand stitch it to the side seam of base for hanging.

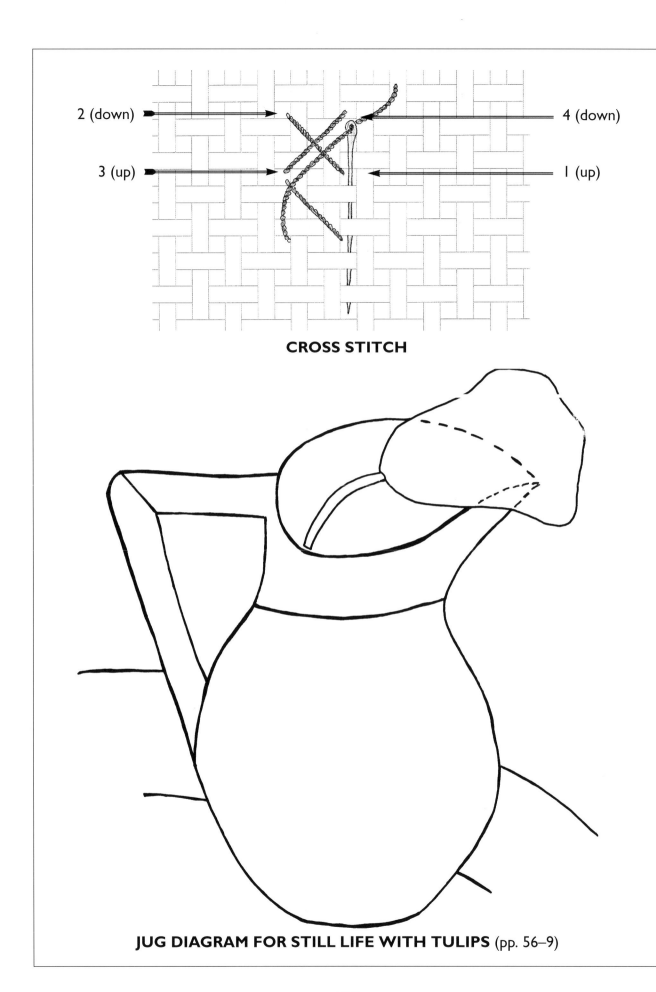

CROSS STITCH

2 (down)

3 (up)

4 (down)

I (up)

JUG DIAGRAM FOR STILL LIFE WITH TULIPS (pp. 56–9)

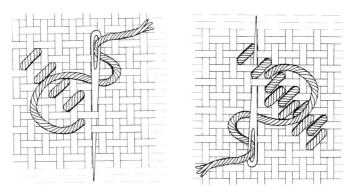

DIAGONAL TENT STITCH

1. Work down first.

2. Fill in the first stitches in the return journey.

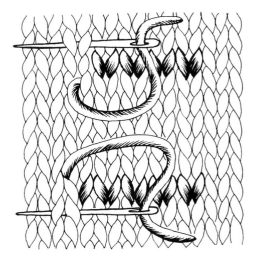

KNITTING STITCH

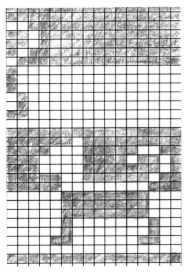

**REPEAT PATTERN
OF DOGS FOR
KNITTING STITCH**
(pp. 84–7)

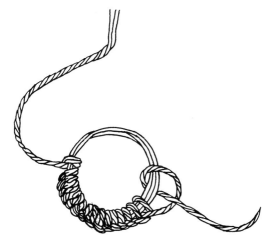

KNOTTED LOOP

KNITTING AND CROCHET ABBREVIATIONS

alt alternate

beg begin/ing

ch chain

cm centimetre/s

cont continue

dc double crochet

dec decrease, decreasing

foll following

garter st knit every row

htr half treble

inc increase, increasing

K knit

M1 make one: pick up the loop which lies before next stitch, place on left hand needle and knit through back of loop

patt pattern

P purl

psso pass slipped stitch over

rem remain/s, remaining

rep repeat

sl slip

st/s stitch/es

sl st slip stitch (crochet)

rev st st reverse stocking stitch: purl row on right side, knit row on wrong side of work

st st stocking stitch: knit row on right side, purl row on wrong side of work

tbl through back of loop

tog together

tr treble

ybk yarn back: take yarn under needle from purling position to knitting position

yfwd yarn forward: bring yarn under needle from knitting position to purling position

C6F sl next 3 sts on a cable needle and leave at front of work, K3 then K3 from cable needle

C6B sl next 3 sts on a cable needle and leave at back of work, K3, then K3 from cable needle

CROCHET TERMS

ENGLISH	AMERICAN
double crochet (dc)	single crochet
treble (tr)	double crochet
half treble (htr)	half double crochet